Gay Believers: Homosexuality and Religion

The Gallup's Guide to Modern Gay, Lesbian, & Transgender Lifestyle

BEING GAY, STAYING HEALTHY

COMING OUT:
TELLING FAMILY AND FRIENDS

FEELING WRONG IN YOUR OWN BODY:
UNDERSTANDING WHAT IT MEANS TO BE TRANSGENDER

GAY AND LESBIAN ROLE MODELS

GAY BELIEVERS:
HOMOSEXUALITY AND RELIGION

GAY ISSUES AND POLITICS:
MARRIAGE, THE MILITARY, & WORK PLACE DISCRIMINATION

GAYS AND MENTAL HEALTH:
FIGHTING DEPRESSION, SAYING NO TO SUICIDE

HOMOPHOBIA:
FROM SOCIAL STIGMA TO HATE CRIMES

HOMOSEXUALITY AROUND THE WORLD:
SAFE HAVENS, CULTURAL CHALLENGES

A NEW GENERATION OF HOMOSEXUALITY:
MODERN TRENDS IN GAY & LESBIAN COMMUNITIES

SMASHING THE STEREOTYPES:
WHAT DOES IT MEAN TO BE GAY,
LESBIAN, BISEXUAL, OR TRANSGENDER?

STATISTICAL TIMELINE AND OVERVIEW OF GAY LIFE

WHAT CAUSES SEXUAL ORIENTATION?
GENETICS, BIOLOGY, PSYCHOLOGY

GAY PEOPLE OF COLOR:
FACING PREJUDICES, FORGING IDENTITIES

GAY CHARACTERS IN THEATER, MOVIES, AND TELEVISION:
NEW ROLES, NEW ATTITUDES

Gay Believers: Homosexuality and Religion

by Emily Sanna

Mason Crest Publishers

MASON CREST PUBLISHERS INC.
370 Reed Road
Broomall, Pennsylvania 19008
(866)MCP-BOOK (toll free)
www.masoncrest.com

First Printing
9 8 7 6 5 4 3 2 1

Library of Congress Cataloging-in-Publication Data
Sanna, Emily.
  Gay believers : homosexuality and religion / by Emily Sanna.
    p. cm. — (The Gallup's guide to modern gay, lesbian, & transgender life-style)
  Includes bibliographical references and index.
   ISBN 978-1-4222-1749-8   ISBN 978-1-4222-1758-0 (series)
   ISBN 978-1-4222-1868-6 (pbk.)   ISBN 978-1-4222-1863-1 (pbk series)
 1. Gays—Religious life. 2. Gays—Religious life--United States. 3. Sex—Religious aspects. 4. Homosexuality—Religious aspects. I. Title.
   HQ75.15.S26 2011
   200.86'64—dc22
                                2010012747

Produced by Harding House Publishing Service, Inc.
www.hardinghousepages.com
Interior design by MK Bassett-Harvey.
Cover design by Torque Advertising + Design.
Printed in the USA by Bang Printing

PICTURE CREDITS

Andreas Tille, Creative Commons:
    p. 27
Creative Commons: pp. 50, 59
Dr. Blofeld, Creative Commons:
    p. 21

Queereaster Media Working Group,
    Creative Commons: p. 11
Three Faiths, One God: p. 41
Yorck Project, Creative Commons: p. 16

Contents

Introduction

We are both individuals and community members. Our differences define individuality; our commonalities create a community. Some differences, like the ability to run swiftly or to speak confidently, can make an individual stand out in a way that is viewed as beneficial by a community, while the group may frown upon others. Some of those differences may be difficult to hide (like skin color or physical disability), while others can be hidden (like religious views or sexual orientation). Moreover, what some communities or cultures deem as desirable differences, like thinness, is a negative quality in other contemporary communities. This is certainly the case with sexual orientation and gender identity, as explained in *Homosexuality Around the World*, one of the volumes in this book series.

Often, there is a tension between the individual (individual rights) and the community (common good). This is easily visible in everyday matters like the right to own land versus the common good of building roads. These cases sometimes result in community controversy and often are adjudicated by the courts.

An even more basic right than property ownership, however, is one's gender and sexuality. Does the right of gender expression trump the concerns and fears of a community or a family or a school? *Feeling Wrong in Your Own Body*, as the author of that volume suggests, means confronting, in the most personal way, the tension between individuality and community. And, while a community, family, and school have the right (and obligation) to protect its children, does the notion of property rights extend to controlling young adults' choice as to how they express themselves in terms of gender or sexuality?

Changes in how a community (or a majority of the community) thinks about an individual right or responsibility often precedes changes in the law enacted by legislatures or decided by courts. And for these changes to occur, individuals (sometimes working in small groups) often defied popular opinion, political pressure, or religious beliefs. Some of these trends are discussed in *A New Generation of Homosexuality*. Every generation (including yours!) stands on the accomplishments of our ancestors and in *Gay and Lesbian Role Models* you'll be reading about some of them.

One of the most pernicious aspects of discrimination on the basis of sexual orientation is that "homosexuality" is a stigma that can be hidden (see the volume about *Homophobia*). While some of my generation (I was your age in the early 1960s) think that life is so much easier being "queer" in the age of the Internet, Gay-Straight Alliances, and Ellen, in reality, being different in areas where difference matters is *always* difficult. Coming Out, as described in the volume of the same title, is always challenging—for both those who choose to come out and for the friends and family they trust with what was once a hidden truth. Being healthy means being honest—at least to yourself. Having supportive friends and family is most important, as explained in *Being Gay, Staying Healthy*.

Sometimes we create our own "families"—persons bound together by love and identity but not by name or bloodline. This is quite common in gay communities today as it was several generations ago. Forming families or small communities based on rejection by the larger community can also be a double-edged sword. While these can be positive, they may also turn into prisons of conformity. Does being lesbian, for example, mean everyone has short hair, hates men, and drives (or rides on) a motorcycle? *What Does It Mean to Be Gay, Lesbian, Bisexual, or Transgender?* "smashes" these and other stereotypes.

Another common misconception is that "all gay people are alike"—a classic example of a stereotypical statement. We may be drawn together because of a common prejudice or oppression, but we should not forfeit our individuality for the sake of the safety of a common identity, which is one of the challenges shown in *Gay People of Color: Facing Prejudices, Forging Identities*.

Coming out to who *you* are is just as important as having a group or "family" within which to safely come out. Becoming knowledgeable about these issues (through the books in this series and the other resources to which they will lead), feeling good about yourself, behaving safely, actively listening to others *and* to your inner spirit—all this will allow you to fulfill your promise and potential.

James T. Sears, PhD
Consultant

chapter 1

Sexual Preference and Religion: What Are the Issues?

Lauren has always loved church. She loves the songs, she loves praying, she loves reading the Bible. Growing up, she loved the feeling she had at church of connecting to God with a group of other people who worshipped Him in the same way.

But Lauren no longer feels that way. As a teenager, she's realized she is a lesbian—and her church has no place in its pews for homosexuals. She can either deny the reality of her sexual preference, or she can leave her church, condemned as a sinner living outside Christ's *salvation*.

What's That Mean?

When Christians speak of *salvation*, they usually mean the deliverance, by the grace of God, from eternal punishment for sin. They believe that this is granted to those who accept by faith certain conditions of repentance and faith in Jesus.

Lauren feels angry and confused. In many ways, she still believes the way she always has. She wants to worship God the way she always has. **Evangelical** Christianity is a part of who she is—but so is being a lesbian. She wants to believe God does not condemn her for her sexual preferences, but at the same time, she doesn't really know how to think about God anymore. Does God believe she is sinner, the way her church does?

"You can't be a Jew and be gay."

That's what Joel's older sister Kate told him, when he confided in her that he thought he was more attracted to other boys than he was to girls.

"So you better get over that right now," Kate continued. "Because if Mom finds out, she'll be really upset."

Joel knew his mother wanted all her kids to get married and give her grandchildren. But his oldest sister Judy was thirty-five, and still didn't have any children, although she was married. Judy was a lawyer, and she said she

What's That Mean?

Evangelical Christianity is a form of Protestant Christianity that began in the 1700s. Evangelicals believe in the need for personal conversion (what they call being "born again"); they believe that most of the Bible's directions are to be taken literally; and they emphasize the importance of the death and resurrection of Jesus.

didn't have time to have children. Their mother disapproved and fretted and complained—but it wasn't that big of a deal. Would it be that much worse if his parents found out he was homosexual?

Two years later, when Joel was seventeen, he finally revealed to his parents that he was gay. They didn't seem angry, only sad and worried. "See, that wasn't so terrible," Joel remembers saying to Kate. "They'll get used to the idea, and then everything will be fine."

"I hope so," was all Kate said.

"Coming out of the closet" is often a stressful process for gay young people, but it can be particularly difficult in religious families.

Two weeks later, Joel's mother announced that she had made an appointment for him to see a psychologist. "He's Jewish," she told Joel, "and he works exclusively with people like you, people who are strugglers."

"Strugglers?" Joel didn't think he needed to see a psychologist, but at this point, he still wasn't expecting what was coming next. He assumed his mom thought a therapist could help him cope with the stress of coming out as a gay Jewish man.

"That's the word the therapist used," his mother said. "People who are trying to overcome their same-sex attraction so that they can live the Jewish faith. He was very positive. He says he's never had a failure, that all his clients are eventually able to get over their homosexual urges and go on to have happy marriages."

The next few weeks were full of tension in Joel's family. His two sisters sided with him and argued with their parents against the decision to send Joel to a therapist. Their father was silent, their mother cried. In the end, Joel went to the appointment with the psychologist.

The man was respectful and pleasant, but Joel was too angry to give him a chance. After a few sessions, though, Joel was starting to feel confused. Maybe the guy was right, maybe he could stop being attracted to other men. Maybe he should. Joel felt guilty and upset.

For weeks, Joel lay awake at night, talking to God in his mind, trying to sort out his confusion. These times of prayer gave him a sense of peace. He felt as though God were the only thing in his life he was sure of now, the only one who understood him, who didn't care what he was. He knew that whatever route he chose, he wanted to keep that connection to God alive in his life.

Eventually, Joel went to talk to his **rabbi**. He felt awkward at first, but eventually, he was able to tell the rabbi his whole story. He finished by saying, "I'm not even sure who I am anymore. If I'm gay, then that apparently means I'm not Jewish. I don't want to lose being Jewish. But at the same time, if being Jewish means I can't be gay . . . well, I'm not sure I can handle that either."

The rabbi said, "First of all, Joel, a Jew is a Jew is a Jew. Your identity as a Jew who is entitled to practice your faith does not depend on your sexual feelings or desires or life-partner choices. It simply is so. So let's start with that as our foundation."

Joel found talking with his rabbi far more helpful than talking to the therapist. Eventually, his parents agreed to talk with the rabbi as well. Joel and his family still haven't found an answer that makes everyone happy, but Joel has a new sense of confidence and clarity, knowing that as a gay man he will also always be a Jew.

What's That Mean?

A *mosque* is a Muslim place of worship.

When Faisal Alam's family moved to the United States when he was ten, they remained as devoted to their religion as they had been in their home country. Attending *mosque* was an important part of Faisal's life; being a Muslim was vital to his identity. But at the same time, even as a child, he knew he "wasn't like other boys."

"One of the things that was taught to me at my mosque was that homosexuality is forbidden within Islam," he told the Lansing, Michigan, *City Pulse*. "There's no such thing as a gay Muslim, because they just don't exist."

On the outside, at least, Faisal was the model Muslim teenager. When he went to college, he represented the Muslim Student Association in the New England region. Meanwhile, in the city's nightclubs, he had "exploded out of the closet."

Faisal entered a relationship with a young woman and became engaged, but they eventually broke up. When they did, Faisal at last faced the fact that he needed to somehow find a way to heal the break between the two parts of his identity—being Muslim and being gay. "They were both part of who I was," he says.

Today Faisal works with other young Muslims who are facing the same issue. He is the leader of Al-Fatiha, an organization dedicated to empowering gay, lesbian, bisexual, and transgender Muslims. "They come to Al-Fatiha trying to find a way back," he says. "It's such a powerful, spiritual experience to be in a space finally that welcomes you as you are. . . ."

Although helping people to reconcile homosexuality with Islam is Faisal's mission in life, he still hasn't completely found his own answers. He doesn't attend mosque, and he considers himself more spiritual than religious. There is still a wound inside him that lies between his gay identity and his Muslim one.

Ekanta looks very much like any American teenager. She wears blue jeans most of the time, and the tiny diamond she wears in her nostril is very fashionable. Her friends tell her that her dark eyes, long shiny hair, and white smile make her beautiful. Boys like her, but Ekanta has never been interested in dating. She liked having fun with her friends, but her religion was always more important to her. "As a Hindu," she says, "I want to give myself to the Divine. I've wanted this ever since I was a little girl, praying with my grandmother in front of Krishna. This means I will seek self-control. I will give myself in service to others. I always assumed that one day I would marry, but I did not intend to allow sexual attachments to divert me from my pursuit of the Truth."

When Ekanta was eighteen, her parents arranged an engagement for her with an Indian businessman from New Delhi who had recently immigrated to the United States. "He was a little older than me, in his thirties, but that was not a concern for me," Ekanta says. "We were quite compatible. I felt sure I could have a happy life with him, because he respected

The god Krishna is portrayed here with blue skin, to indicate his divinity, being adored by young women.

my devotion to my religion. I wanted to go to college, though, so we agreed to wait until I graduated to marry."

At college, however, Ekanta fell in love for the first time—with another woman. "Suddenly," she says, "my whole life has changed. Homosexuality is not the issue so much. For me and my family, homosexuality is an external trait that has nothing to do with

EXTRA INFO

Many Hindus worship the god Krishna—but Hindus see him in different ways. For some, he is a manifestation of the Supreme Being, while for others, he is the Supreme Being. He is also seen as a child, a lover, and hero, and a prankster.

your spirit. The *guna*—the character and personality traits—of a person are much more important than any label. If I tell my parents I am a lesbian, they will not be upset with me or condemn me, but they will still expect me to get married. They will not understand why I would not want to now. And what bothers me is that I can no longer look at myself the same. In my heart, I thought I was better than my friends who were always falling in love. I had more control, I was not mired in sexual feelings like they were, I had risen above the physical plain to

What's That Mean?

Transgender has to do with identifying with a different gender identity from the one that corresponds with a person's sex at birth. In other words, a person who was born male would have a feminine identity; a person born female would have a masculine identity.

Liberal means open to change and new ideas.

a purer devotion to the god. And now I am faced to admit that is not true. I am a lesbian. It was only because I had not faced that fact that I thought I was so sexually pure. This is upsetting and confusing to me. I do not want to give up my pursuit of Truth. I do not want to give up my lover. I do not know how to put the two together. I do not know if it is possible."

Sunee was born in Thailand and lived there until she was seventeen. Although Sunee has a penis, she thinks of herself as a girl. She has long hair, wears dresses, and carefully puts on her makeup every morning. In Thailand, Sunee was accepted as being a member of the third sex, sometimes referred to as a kathoey. She had seen herself as female for as long as she could remember, and her family considered her a girl as well. As devout Buddhists, Sunee's *trangender* identity had never been an issue for them.

When the family moved to the United States, however, all that changed. Sunee had expected American to be more *liberal*, but that turned out not to be the case. She had to register for high school as a boy, and word quickly spread that the new Thai girl was actually male. People whispered and giggled behind her back. Unfortunately, Sunee spoke English well enough that she could understand what they were saying. She came home and cried in her room every day.

EXTRA INFO

Arranged marriages are still common practice in many traditional families from India and other parts of Asia. In these cultures, couples do not get to know each other through dating; instead, parents search for compatible partners for their children. These families, including the young adults involved, view this as completely normal and acceptable. As the world becomes more Westernized, some young adults from these cultures are beginning to date, but they still tend to view arranged marriages as an option they can fall back on if they are unable or unwilling to spend the time and effort necessary to find spouses on their own.

Sunee and her mother went to a Buddhist temple to ask the advice of a priest. He told them, "Everyone has been a member of the third sex in a past life—so the people who are laughing at you were once themselves just like you in another life. All of us have been through innumerable cycles of **reincarnation**. No one can know how many times they have been like you in the past or how many times they will be in the future. To be born as a member of the third sex is the consequence of how we lived a past life."

"So it is punishment for bad **karma**?" Sunee's mother asked.

The priest nodded, and Sunee's heart sank. "But," he said, "it is not bad karma to live your life as the third sex. It is simply God's will for you in this life. There is no future punishment for it."

What's That Mean?

Reincarnation **is the belief that souls are reborn in new bodies, again and again until they reach enlightenment.**

Karma **is the force recognized by both Hindus and Buddhists that is created by people's actions in this life, which in turn determines where they end up in their next lives.**

After that, Sunee was still unhappy at school, and she did not like thinking that her very identity was punishment for her past sins. "But in some ways," she says, "I did feel better."

When she graduated from high school, she attended Oberlin College, where her transgender identity was once more recognized and affirmed. She is resolved now to have the surgery that will change her physically into a woman, and her parents support her decision. She wants to go on to become a doctor, and she hopes that one day she will find a man to marry who will accept her. In the meantime, she says, "My faith gives me strength and peace every day."

All these five young people have something important in common: they are all deeply committed to a life of faith. They do not want to live their lives apart from their spiritual beliefs. Their faith is essential not only to how they understand their lives but to their very identities as well. But these individuals also have something else in common: they are all struggling to reconcile their sexual and gender issues with their faith.

The Buddhist Wheel of Life portrays the concept of life, death, and rebirth, with karma being the force that drives a person from one level of the cycle to another.

What's That Mean?

Scriptures are holy writings. They are often very ancient. Religious texts, also known as scripture, are the texts which various religious traditions consider to be sacred, or of central importance to their religious tradition. Many religions and spiritual movements believe their sacred texts are divinely or supernaturally inspired (in other words, God or some other supernatural force gave the message directly to the human authors).

Jews consider the Tanakh or Miqra, which include the Five Books of Moses (the Torah), the Prophets, and the Writings, to be scripture. The Christians include the Jewish scriptures in what they call the Old Testament; with the New Testament, these scriptures make up the Christian Bible. Hindus have many sacred scriptures, which were passed along orally for thousands of years before they were written; some of the most important are called the Vedas and the Upanishads. Buddhists also have several groups of scripture, including the Sutras (the words of Buddha), the Pali Canon, and the Tibetan Book of the Dead.

Historically, most cultures have believed that homosexual and transgender behaviors are sinful, and that a lifestyle built on such behaviors separates a person from God, as well as from the rest of the religious community Sacred *scriptures* seemed to support this viewpoint.

As our modern culture changes, however, and homosexuality has become more acceptable, more and more gays and transgenders are refusing to accept that they have to give up their faith. They are taking a fresh look at ancient scriptures and finding that new interpretations are possible. They are starting to ask difficult questions about the difference between faith and culture, between God's perspectives and human perspectives. These are not easy questions to answer.

The issues are a little different for each religious tradition. Even within each faith, different religious groups believe different things. It can be confusing for the individual to find answers, still more confusing to recognize the answers that are right for each individual.

Find Out More on the Internet

Homosexuality and Religion Resources
hirr.hartsem.edu/research/homosexuality_religion.html

Religious Tolerance
www.religioustolerance.org/hom_chur.htm

Read More About It

De la Juerta, Christian. *Coming Out Spiritually: The Next Step*. New York: Tarcher, 2009.

Johnson, Toby. *Gay Spirituality*. Maple Shade, N.J.: Lethe Press, 2004.

Runzo, Joseph and Nancy M. Martin. *Love, Sex, and Gender in the World Religions*. Oxford, U.K.: One World Publications, 2000.

chapter 2

Christianity

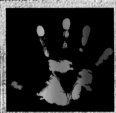

What's That Mean?

The word *"Catholic"* was first used in the sixteenth century to refer to the form of Christianity led by the Pope in Rome, whose authority was supported by layers of bishops and priests. Unlike Protestants, who usually stress the importance of scripture as the only religious authority, Catholics also recognize the authority of tradition as it has been handed down by the leaders of the Catholic Church.

Historically, the beliefs of the church regarding homosexuality have been built on what was understood to be the teachings of the Bible, particularly the Old Testament. In reality, until the fall of Rome in 430, urban culture at least was tolerant of gay Christians. Not until the organized form of the *Catholic* Church arrived on the scene did Christians become obsessed with sexual sin.

The Catholic Church
HISTORICAL CATHOLICISM

The Catholic Church has a long history of distrusting sexuality, whatever its form. In the Middle Ages (the European era that began around 1000 and ended with the sixteenth century), sexual corruption within the church led to its leaders mandating that priests had to be *celibate*. Sexual urges were viewed as irrational, destructive—and ultimately sinful—desires, on the same level with anger and greed. *Lay people* were allowed to marry, and sex was permissible within the boundary lines drawn by marriage, but only for the purposes of creating babies.

Medieval monks were expected to live quiet lives of prayer and study, separated from the "sinful" temptations of sexual desire.

As a result, Catholicism spoke out strongly and vehemently against all other sexual acts that could not lead to a pregnancy. These included anal sex, oral sex, sex that takes place using any form of birth control—and homosexual intercourse.

CATHOLICISM TODAY

The official teachings of the Church regarding homosexuality have changed very little over the years. Homosexuality itself is not regarded as a sin, since the Catholic Church believes this is not something the individual chooses but rather something with which he or she is born. Any homosexual activities, however, are viewed as evil, since they do not produce babies.

There is often a wide gap between the official stance of the **Vatican** and what is believed by practicing Catholics, especially in the United States. According to a recent Gallup poll, 80 percent of American Catholics believe that individuals should not depend on the Church's teachings but must determine for themselves whether homosexuality is moral or immoral.

Many Catholics, including leading **theologians**, have come to believe that sex is a gift from God,

What's That Mean?

The *Vatican* is the small city where the Pope lives in Rome, Italy and is the seat of authority in the Catholic Church.

intended not only to produce babies but also as an expression of intimacy and committed love. Abusive or demeaning sexual relationships are not what God intended, so sex should be considered a serious and sacred responsibility. Casual sex is not endorsed by this perspective, but any form of **monogamous** sex that expresses the love between two people would be considered to be a gift from God.

The Vatican, a tiny state within the city of Rome, Italy, is the governing center of the Catholic Church, and Catholicism's official stance on homosexuality is issued from here. Not all Catholics, however, agree with all of their church's formal teachings.

What's That Mean?

Protestants are members of the Western Christian church whose faith and practice are founded on the principles of the Reformation (the sixteenth-century movement that led to many Christians breaking away from the Catholic Church), especially in the acceptance of the Bible as the only religious authority, in salvation by faith alone, and in the universal priesthood of all believers.

A hierarchy organizes things—or people—in layers of importance, with those at the top having the most status or importance.

Denominations are large groups of religious congregations united under a common faith and name, and organized under a single legal administration.

The Protestant Viewpoint

Unlike Catholicism, *Protestants* have no single unifying *hierarchy*. There are many Protestant *denominations*, and each one looks at homosexuality a little differently. For example, the United Church of Christ has an official perspective similar to many Catholics' unofficial beliefs. Since homosexuality is not something a person chooses for herself, it cannot be a sin. Homosexual activity should be guided by the same moral rules that apply to heterosexual sex (such as monogamy, faithfulness, etc.). Meanwhile, many Presbyterians and Lutherans oppose homosexuality on moral grounds while they actively affirm the civil rights of *LGBT* people. Many of these churches are politically active, working to end discrimination against same-sex couples. The Church of the Brethren takes a similar stand. Other Protestant denominations, such as the Unity and Universalist churches, believe there is nothing wrong with homosexuality, and that homosexuals have the right to be married within the church.

The issue of same-sex marriages is a dividing factor for many Protestant groups. Methodists believe in the rights of LGBT to be married in civil unions, but they are divided over whether or not clergy should perform marriages. Many Episcopalians believe that homosexuals and same-sex marriages should not only be accepted but welcomed and blessed by the church. Other Episcopalians strongly disagree, and the issue has threatened to split their church.

The **ordination** of openly gay people is another issue with which Protestant denominations struggle. The most liberal denominations, those that perform same-sex marriages (such as the Unitarians and the United Church of Christ) have for some time ordained gays. Some, like the Episcopalians, are moving toward full inclusion of gays at all levels of their

What's That Mean?

LGBT stands for lesbian, gay, bisexual, and transgender. It's a collection of letters that's often used to cover with a single term the whole spectrum of gender and sexual differences.

Ordination is the process of becoming a member of the clergy.

hierarchy. Others, such as the Methodists and Presbyterians, continue to debate the issue. Many gay people serve as ministers in these and all denominations, and must wait patiently for their churches to come to terms with their official recognition.

And then at the other end of the spectrum are *conservative*, Evangelical churches that are actively against all forms of homosexuality. These groups believe that homosexuality is both a choice and a sin. Most of these groups would teach that it is wrong to treat a gay person unkindly, but they would say that homosexuals need to be saved from their sin. This perspective is expressed well by theologian Lehman Strauss:

What's That Mean?

Someone who is *conservative* favors traditional values and views, and tends to resist change.

We must always keep before us the fact that homosexuals, like all of us sinners, are the objects of God's love. The Bible says, "But God commendeth His love toward us, in that while we were yet sinners, Christ died for us" (Romans 5:8). . . . The Christian who shares God's love for lost sinners will seek to reach the homosexual with the gospel of Christ, which "is the power of God unto salvation, to every one that believeth" (Romans 1:16). As a Christian I should hate all sin but I can find no justification for hating the sinner. The homosexual is a precious soul for whom Christ died. We Christians can show him the best way of life by pointing him to Christ.

Unfortunately, prejudice sometimes uses Christianity to justify itself, but that is true of most religions. When that happens—when prejudice clothes itself in religion—the true faith, the central meaning that is taught in its scriptures, is distorted, if not corrupted. Ultimately, despite their conflicting viewpoints, most Christians are sincerely struggling to interact with the modern world in a spirit of love, being true to what they believe God wants. Their viewpoints on homosexuality, however, differ so much that this issue has become a line that sharply separates groups of Christians, interfering with the unity they claim in the spirit of Christ.

Find Out More on the Internet

Christianity and Homosexuality (an Evangelical perspective)
home.messiah.edu/ ~ chase/h/

Homosexuality and Christianity (a liberal perspective)
www.jeramyt.org/gay.html

Read More About It

Cannon, Justin R. *The Bible, Christianity, and Homosexuality.* New York: Create Space, 2008.

Moore, Gareth. *A Question of Truth: Christianity and Homosexuality.* New York: Continuum, 2003.

Rogers, Jack. *Jesus, the Bible, and Homosexuality: Explode the Myths, Heal the Church.* Louisville, KY: Westminster John Knox, 2009.

chapter 3

Judaism

Judaism believes that sexuality is a powerful force that can be used both for good and for evil. Therefore, sexuality needs to be channeled carefully. Although procreation is seen as the primary purpose of sex (as with Christianity), Judaism recognizes that sexual intimacy is a healthy source of pleasure.

Historical Judaism and Homosexuality

Traditionally, Judaism has been against homosexuality. In the scriptures, sexual acts such as incest, masturbation, and homosexuality are often grouped together as unacceptable, and the **halakah**

What's That Mean?

The *halakah* are the Jewish rules or laws that have been handed down to guide everyday behavior, often based on an interpretation of the Torah (the books of law, also called the Five Books of Moses, in the Jewish scripture).

specifically prohibits same-sex relationships. In later *rabbinic* writings, male homosexuality is condemned, both because it doesn't result in children and because it is viewed as a selfish activity that only gives pleasure to one partner at a time. Male-male intercourse is referred to as an "abhorrence" in the Jewish scriptures.

Meanwhile, the ancient Jewish laws say much less about lesbianism. Since no penetration occurs during female-female sex, women who had had sexual relationships with other women were still considered virgins. This meant they were "pure" and could marry priests.

In general, the Jewish religion treated women as though they were so insignificant as to be invisible; as a result, lesbian relationships were largely ignored. At most, they were referred to as an "obscenity" (a much milder word than "abhorrence"!), but only because lesbian sex involved the woman exposing her naked body to another woman.

What's That Mean?

Rabbinic has to do with the teachings and writings of the rabbis, down through the centuries.

Trivializing means making something seem unimportant.

Modern Judaism and Homosexuality

Today, some Jewish women argue that by ignoring female homosexuals, Judaism is *trivializing* lesbianism, that in effect, to be a lesbian Jew is to be ignored, to have your experience *invalidated*. "How can you embrace a religion where your central experience is dismissed as merely a minor infraction?" asks one woman.

As with Christianity, different Jewish groups look at homosexuality differently. Orthodox Jews still hold on to the traditional perspectives on homosexuality. This means that if a person comes out as gay, he may very well have to leave his religious community and become estranged from his family. Meanwhile

EXTRA INFO

The largest Jewish groups are Orthodox Judaism, Conservative Judaism, and Reform Judaism. A major difference between these groups is their approach to Jewish law: Orthodox and Conservative Judaism believe that Jewish law should be followed, with Conservative Judaism promoting a more "modern" interpretation than Orthodox Judaism; Reform Judaism is generally more liberal than these other two movements, viewing Jewish law as a set of general guidelines rather than as a list of restrictions whose literal observance is required.

within Conservative Judaism, LGBT Jews are generally accepted, but while some groups within Conservative Judaism ordain gay rabbis and even perform same-sex blessings, others do not or will only ordain gay rabbis who will commit to being celibate. Some

EXTRA INFO

The story of Ruth and Naomi is told in the book of Ruth, which is contained within both the Jewish and Christian scriptures. Naomi is Ruth's mother-in-law, but both their husbands have died. When Naomi decides to go back to her homeland, she tells Ruth to return to her own family as well—but Ruth responds, "Don't ask me to ever leave you . . . for only death will separate me from you."

Conservative Jews also believe that it is not male-male sex that is prohibited in the Torah, but only anal sex; in that case, male homosexual relationships would be allowed, so long as the homosexual partners engaged in sexual activity that did not include anal intercourse. Within Reform Judaism, gays and lesbians are respected, openly gay people are ordained as rabbis, and Reform rabbis perform commitment ceremonies between gay and lesbian couples. Despite their liberal stance on gay marriage, some Reform Jews still have some discomfort with people who identify as bisexual. They can accept that homosexuality may be a variation of God's plan, since homosexuals have no choice in the matter. But, they believe, if you are attracted to both genders, you should choose to be "normal."

Many liberal Jews are taking another look at scriptures and finding new meanings in many of the stories. The story of Ruth and Naomi, for example, is viewed as an example of committed love between two women.

For most Jews who accept homosexuality, monogamy is the more important issue. They believe that God created the sex act to be a joyful expression of committed love between two people, regardless of their gender.

FIND OUT MORE ON THE INTERNET

The History of Homosexuality and Judaism
www.religionfacts.com/homosexuality/judaism.htm

Jewish Law and Homosexuality
www.jlaw.com/Commentary/homosexuality.html

READ MORE ABOUT IT

Brown, Angela. *Mentsh: On Being Jewish and Queer*. Los Angeles: Alyson, 2004.

Rapoport, Chaim. *Judaism and Homosexuality: An Authentic Orthodox View*. Edgware, U.K.: Mitchell Vallentine, 2004.

chapter 4

 # Islam

The Qur'an, or Muslim holy book, clearly condemns homosexuality. Many traditional Muslims connect this issue to the story of Lot (a story that also appears in Christian and Jewish scriptures). In the story, God lets Lot leave his home in the town of Sodom before it is destroyed. In Muslim (as well as Christian) tradition, the city is destroyed because the people in it are practicing homosexuality. For this reason, gays and lesbians are referred to as *Luti*, or "Lot's people." The story of Lot is mentioned five times throughout the Qur'an.

Part of the reason why Islam views homosexuality as sinful is that sex is understood to be for the purpose of procreation—for making children. Sexual activity is therefore encouraged and even sacred; there is no tradition of celibacy in Islam as there is in Christianity or other religions.

Homosexuality in Modern Islamic Culture

Today, homosexuality remains punishable by *shari'a*, Islamic law. In some Muslim countries, the punishment is a death sentence. However, solid evidence must be provided before punishment occurs, and most Muslims aren't that concerned with what others do in their private lives. As long as homosexuality occurs in private, realistically, it cannot be punished.

This affects how people in the Islamic world, and even Muslims here in the United States, label themselves. As a Muslim, it's not so bad to have sex with someone of the same gender, as long as you don't proclaim yourself as gay, and take on a homosexual identity.

Many conservative Muslims see the label of "homosexuality" as a sign of Western culture and its influence on Islamic ways of life. These people

According to Muslim tradition (as well as Christian), God rained down fire on the ancient city of Sodom because its inhabitants were practicing homosexuality.

would argue that there was no label before the West got involved—people did what they wanted in private, but they would eventually become part of a heterosexual marriage, and no one felt the need to proclaim themselves as "gay."

This understanding of homosexual behavior has both its pros and cons. On the plus side, it frees people to act however they want in private, as long as they are able to conform to Muslim codes of behavior in public. But many gay Muslims, especially in the United States, feel that pretending a part of them doesn't exist is not an acceptable way to live. Keep-

EXTRA INFO

In Mohammed's "Farewell Sermon" (Mohammed was the founder of Islam), he says that a man who engages in homosexual sex will "appear on the Last Day stinking worse than a corpse . . . and God will cancel all his good deeds." However, there is no such lasting punishment for women who engage in homosexual acts.

ing up a public appearance of heterosexuality, they say, denies that a part of them really exists.

Now that the Gay Rights movements and other Western influences have gained so much attention all around the world, Muslims who are gay or bisexual are beginning to be proud of their identities. They want to come out of the closet—or they feel that they *should* come out—and when they do, they run into trouble with the traditions of their religious background.

Islam and the Issue of Gay Marriage

If homosexuality is evil according to the Qur'an—in fact, it is so bad that God destroyed an entire town over homosexual behavior!—then same-gender marriage is not a possibility for many Muslims. Instead, they believe that because the purpose of a marriage

The traditional family is very important to Muslim belief.

is to produce children, a true marriage can only exist between a man and a woman.

However, many liberal Muslims are reinterpreting other passages in the Scripture that seem to point to a more *inclusive* idea of relationships, and they use these as a justification for gay marriage. For example, in some parts of the *Qur'an* that talk about the nature of relationships between people, the word used—*zaui*—is not gendered; instead, it means one half of a partnership. This word has been used to argue for the equality of both the man and the woman in a heterosexual relationship, as well as for the understanding that human partnerships can be between people of both different and the same gender.

What's That Mean?

Inclusive means that something includes as much as possible within its boundaries. A person who is inclusive interacts with everyone without paying attention to differences.

Gay and Lesbian Muslims in the United States

In the 2008 San Francisco Gay Pride parade, for the first time there was a Muslim float. However, unlike the rest of the crowd, who were openly embracing their identities as LGBT people, these Muslim gay men hid behind sunglasses and hats. While Islam tends to be more liberal in the United States than in

Muslim countries like Egypt or Afghanistan, it is still hard for American Muslims to come out and publically proclaim a homosexual identity.

However, this is slowly changing. Many Muslim **advocates** for gay rights argue that the *Qur'an* emphasizes that all people are God's creation. Everyone is equally loved and cared for by God, no matter what their sexuality. Some people also argue that while the *Qur'an* forbids "abominations" when it comes to same-sex relations, it is never clear what these abominations are. All scripture is open to interpretation, and the *Qur'an* can be interpreted in a more inclusive light. Other homosexual Muslims draw on alternative traditions within Islam and rely less on Scripture and Islamic Law. One such tradition is Sufism, a **mystical** tradition within Islam that stresses personal experience and relationship with God.

What's That Mean?

Advocates are people who stand up on behalf of something or someone.

Mystical has to do with a religious perspective that pursues a conscious awareness of God—or of an ultimate reality—through direct experience or insight.

Transgender Issues within Islam

Islam has not as a whole dealt directly with transgender issues. The one passage in an Islamic religious text that seems to touch on the issue is a hadith (a story about the Prophet Mohammed) that seems to argue against cross-dressing, saying that "cursed are those men who wear women's clothing and those women who wear men's clothing." Another *hadith* condemns "the **hermaphrodites** among the man and the over-masculine women." However, despite these two stories, transgender issues are actually understood and accepted within Islam more than homosexuality is.

In 1988, Islamic law declared that surgery to change a person's gender was an acceptable surgery for transgender individuals. In Egypt, the highest religious leader in the country issued a decree that gender-reassignment surgery was permissible and even encouraged in cases where a patient was truly transgender and unable to live a full life as the gender into which they had been born. However, the decree went on to proclaim, surgery for the mere wish of changing sex is not permitted.

What's That Mean?

Hermaphrodites are people (or animals) that have both male and female sex organs.

Other Muslim countries have also responded positively toward transgender individuals. In Malaysia, the government has accepted transgender people for years and will reissue any government documents in people's new gender identities. In 2004, Iran officially recognized transgenders, also allowing them to have sex-reassignment surgery and to get new official documents.

Islam is often considered as a whole to be one of the more conservative religions. However, within the Muslim tradition people are slowly finding ways to integrate both their religious identity and their identities as LGBT individuals, whether this means separating their public from their private lives, reinterpreting the *Qur'an*, or drawing on alternative traditions.

FIND OUT MORE ON THE INTERNET

Al Faitha
www.al-fatiha.org

American Islamic Fellowship
www.americanislamicfellowship.org

Safra Project
safraproject.org

READ MORE ABOUT IT

Habib, Samar, ed. *Islam and Homosexuality*. New York: Praeger, 2009.

Kugel, Scott. *Homosexuality in Islam: Islamic Reflection on Gay, Lesbian, and Transgender Muslims*. Oxford, U.K.: Oneworld, 2010.

chapter 5

Hinduism and Homosexuality

According to Harvard University's Pluralism Project, more than 1.2 million Hindus live in the United States today. However, although 1.2 million Americans may call themselves practicing Hindus, this label includes a vast range of beliefs. Unlike the monotheistic religions—Christianity, Judaism, and Islam—Hinduism has no central doctrine that tells people what to believe. Some Hindus believe in many gods, while others believe in no god at all. Some practice daily meditation, while others offer sacrifices, called *pujas*, to their household images of the gods. Some believe that sexuality is an important part of human experience, while others tend more toward asceticism, the practice of giving up all bodily pleasures. For this reason, discussing Hinduism and homosexuality can be difficult, since every Hindu practitioner has her own ideas about what Hinduism is.

The Laws of Manu

The Laws of Manu are a collection of teachings written in India sometime between 200 BCE and 200 CE. They deal with people's *dharma*, or duty; every individual, depending on gender and **caste**, had a specific *dharma* he had to fulfill. The Laws of Manu describe these duties and list appropriate punishments for failing to obey them—and under these laws, homosexuality is considered a crime.

However, some modern Hindus and scholars argue that the punishments were light—and that therefore homosexuality obviously wasn't considered to be all that terrible. For example, if two men were caught engaging in homosexual behavior, they were sentenced to bathe with their clothes on—a punishment that seems uncomfortable, possibly embarrassing, but hardly the end of the world. Sexual acts between two women were seen in a stricter light; the punishment for an older woman engaging in sexual relations with a virgin was to have her head shaved, two fingers cut off, and to ride through town

What's That Mean?

Caste is a Hindu hereditary social class. If you are born into a low caste—or a high caste—that will be your status for your entire life. Although the caste system is weakening in Hindu culture, it is still uncommon for people to marry outside their own caste.

on a donkey. However, some people argue that the severity of that particular punishment had more to do with the one woman being a virgin, since women had be kept pure for marriage, whether the sexual acts in question were between two women or a women and a man.

While homosexuality was cautioned against in laws, many Hindu traditions also allow for a degree of flexibility in sexuality and gender. This can be seen in religious stories and myths. For example, in many Hindu religious traditions, one's *kama*, or bodily pleasure, is seen as equally important as one's duty, or *dharma*. In the *Kama Sutra*, an ancient book that provides directions for embracing one's *kama*, sexual behavior, whether between individuals of the same or different genders, was seen as both enjoyable and meaningful.

Hindu Myths and Legends

The ancient stories of the Hindu gods and goddesses remain important for practicing Hindus today. While the laws of Hinduism might show homosexuality as something that should be avoided or punished, these stories are an alternative source that helps Hindus understand sexuality and gender roles in a much less rigid way.

In one story, Siva, one of the main gods in Hinduism, is trying to have a child with his wife, Parvati. Because he is so spiritual, however, he is unable to get

EXTRA INFO

You may think that gender and sexuality mean the same thing—but actually, they are two different things. According to the World Health Organization:

"Sex" refers to the biological and physiological characteristics that define men and women.

"Gender" refers to the socially constructed roles, behaviors, activities, and attributes that a society considers appropriate for men and women.

To put it another way: "Male" and "female" are sex categories, while "masculine" and "feminine" are gender categories.

Aspects of sex will not vary substantially between different human societies, while aspects of gender may vary greatly.

EXAMPLES OF SEX CHARACTERISTICS

- Women menstruate while men do not.
- Men have testicles while women do not.
- Women have developed breasts that can produce milk for babies, while men have not.
- Men generally have heavier bones than women.

EXAMPLES OF GENDER CHARACTERISTICS

- In the United States (and most other countries), women earn significantly less money than men for similar work.
- In much of the Western world, women can wear dresses while men do not.
- In Saudi Arabia men are allowed to drive cars while women are not.
- In most of the world, women do more housework than men.

his wife pregnant. Eventually, the other gods decide to intervene. Agni, the male god of fire, takes the form of a dove and swallows the seed of Siva. After a long and roundabout story involving artificial insemination and the Ganges River, Kartikkeya, the god of war, is eventually born as a result of the sexual act between Agni and Siva. Thus a sexual act between two males leads to creation and a new expression of the **divine**.

What's That Mean?

When people talk about the *divine* they are referring to God or something that has to do with God.

Hinduism sees physical love as both meaningful and pleasurable, whether it is between same or different genders.

In another story, two widows give birth to a male child. Again, this is not seen as being sinful or in any way negative. The gods bless the widows' relationship, and the child grows up to be a hero.

Today, stories like these provide an important resource for any Hindu person who is also dealing with LGBT issues. The stories show that there is more than one way of looking at sexuality—that sexuality can be creative and sacred, whether it is heterosexual or homosexual.

Being Hindu and Gay

Many modern Hindus believe that homophobia was something that was introduced into their religion by other cultures, especially the British back in the 1700s when they colonized India. Before that time, homosexuality was rarely dealt with in public, but it was a common understanding that heterosexuality was not the only way to live. When the British came to India, however, they instituted rigid punishments for homosexual acts; in the Indian Penal Code, which was written by the British, "carnal intercourse against the order of nature" is still punishable by life in prison.

Today, devout Hindus regard sexuality in several different ways. One popular view argues that physical desires, whether homosexual or heterosexual, are to be avoided. Physical desire leads to a continuation of rebirths, or reincarnation. From this perspective, since the goal of existence is to escape the world we live in now and to move past this cycle of reincarnation, one must escape the need for physical pleasure. This concept is not easy for mainstream Americans to grasp. Hindus who follow this path believe that all the things we own and all our relationships are really meaningless; they tie us down to this material world, and so we should learn to view them as unimportant. In our *materialistic* society, this viewpoint may make little sense, but a positive aspect of this worldview is that souls are not seen as male or female; instead, everyone is equal. Many Hindus, when asked about the definition of marriage, will say that marriage is the union of two souls—and since souls aren't male or female, what does it matter if the marriage is between two women or two men?

What's That Mean?

Something (or someone) that is *materialistic* values material things—such as possessions and money.

The Third Sex

In Hindu culture, every person is considered to have both male and female parts to their personalities. Some men, however, embody more of the "feminine"—and those men are seen as neither male nor female. Members of this "third sex" are referred to in India as *hijra*. Some of the *hijra* are born with both male and female sexual organs, while others were born male, and a few others are males who have undergone surgical procedures. Whatever sex they were born, all of the *hijra* wear traditional women's clothing and use feminine pronouns (like she, her, and hers) to describe themselves.

In traditional Indian society, the *hijra* occupy specific roles. They often perform at births and mar-

EXTRA INFO

The film *Fire* came out in India in 1996 and led to riots by fundamentalist Hindus. The movie portrays two women in a lesbian relationship, and conservative Hindus argued that not only was it wrong to promote lesbian love, but that the film was poking fun at Hinduism itself, since the main characters—Sita and Radha—were both named after important Hindu deities. However, LGBT activists argued that the film didn't go far enough in portraying lesbian issues for Indian women. They complained that the movie implied that lesbians were women who were unfulfilled sexually in their heterosexual relationships and that homosexuality was something that had been brought to India by the British—that rather than being a basic human condition, being gay stemmed from listening to Western music or wearing blue jeans.

riages. It is important to pay the *hijras* well; if they bless a child, he will be successful in life, but anyone who is cursed by a *hijra* will be unlucky.

What's That Mean?

Sects are subdivisions of larger religious groups that usually differ in some way from the rest of the religion.

In some Hindu *sects*, transvestitism (cross-dressing) is a way to show devotion to the god. Men will dress up as women to simulate marriage to Siva. In cases like this, both homosexual behavior and transvestitism is seen as honoring the gods.

FIND OUT MORE ON THE INTERNET

The Gay and Lesbian Vaishnava Association, Inc.
www.galva108.org/index.html

Homosexuality and Hinduism: Religion Facts
www.religionfacts.com/homosexuality/hinduism.htm

READ MORE ABOUT IT

Vanita, Ruth and Saleem Kidwai, eds. *Same-Sex Love in India*. :
Palgrave Macmillan, 2001.

chapter 6

Buddhism

Buddhism developed from Hinduism, and like Hinduism, it has no overarching authority in terms of an organized religious institution or doctrine. The practices and beliefs of Buddhists differ from country to country, as well as between different branches of the religion. This means that a Buddhist in the United States might have different beliefs and religious practices from a Buddhist in Thailand, India, or China.

In many Buddhist contexts, homosexuality has been pretty much a non-issue. Because until recently Buddhism was a religion that was mostly practiced by people outside the United States, the people who practiced the religion didn't think about sexuality the same way Americans do; even the term "homosexuality" implied practices and behaviors that often weren't present in cultures where Buddhism was prevalent.

Instead, one of the main conflicts in Buddhism is sexuality versus celibacy. Many Buddhists believe that a **monastic** life, where a person is entirely celibate, is the ideal, a state of being that leads more easily to Buddhism's goal: ridding yourself of all desire (much like in some branches of Hinduism). From this perspective, all sex and sexual desire (whether heterosexual or homosexual) only leads you away from this goal. While sex is considered necessary and important for those not in religious orders, monks and nuns are forbidden to engage in sexual behavior of any kind, either heterosexual or homosexual. However, the punishment for homosexual acts is not serious, and involves doing **penance**, rather than being expelled entirely from the religious community.

Historical Buddhism and Homosexuality

The *jatakas*, one of the Buddhist sacred writings, are stories about the Buddha's life that teach his followers

What's That Mean?

Monastic has to do with a way of life where people live in seclusion, take religious vows, and follow a fixed set of rules regulating how they spend their time. Men are known as monks and women are known as nuns. Christians (Catholics and Episcopalians), Buddhists, and Hindus all have monastic orders. Although the details will differ from religion to religion, the common goal of all monastic groups is to achieve greater spiritual purity by withdrawing from the world's distractions.

Penance is an act performed to show sorrow for sin or wrongdoing.

how to act. Today, many people argue that some of the *jataka* stories imply that Buddha and some of his companions had a homosexual relationship; for example, one of Buddha's followers, Ananda, is his constant companion and adviser. Whether or not the

EXTRA INFO

Buddhism's main beliefs are expressed in the Four Noble Truths. These facts about life, passed down from the Buddha, state that:

1. *Life is suffering*. Life is hard because humans are imperfect beings. We are mortal, we get sick, people we love die. It is impossible to get through life without losing something or someone we care about.
2. *Suffering is caused by attachment*. If we didn't care about anything, we wouldn't have to feel pain of any kind.
3. *It is possible to end suffering though disattachment*. If we can let go of all our attachments, then we will have no more reason to suffer
4. *The way to achieve this is through the Eight-Fold Path*. The Eight-Fold Path describes exactly how to go about achieving an end to attachment and therefore an end to the soul's constant reincarnation.

Buddha and Ananda were actually engaged in a sexual relationship, the *jatakas* portray same-sex friendships and intimacy as better than relationships with members of the opposite sex. Relationships between men and women can lead to them leaving the religious orders and becoming confused in their pursuit of enlightenment, but same-sex relationships, whether sexual or nonsexual, do not tempt people to leave a community, nor do they result in a family (which was seen as a lesser state than being the member of a religious community). This is very different from the Christian and Jewish perspectives!

What's That Mean?

Homoerotic has to do with homosexual love and desire.

In a monastery, *novices* are people who have entered but not yet taken final vows.

So, at worst, Buddhism was neutral toward homosexuality, while at best it actively encouraged it. As a result, in some branches of Buddhism, homosexuality was practiced regularly. In Japan, for example, a tradition of **homoerotic** literature and poetry dates back to the fourteenth century CE. In these stories, older monks took younger **novices** as lovers as a way to teach the young monks about the practices of their religion. Clearly, from this perspective, homosexuality was not perceived as either sinful or destructive.

Buddhism and Transgender Issues

Because Buddhism views our physical life on Earth as something temporary and inferior, both male and female characteristics are considered to be things that will pass away with our present bodies. People's souls are gender-less. They just happen to be housed in a body with a specific sex. As a result, like in Hinduism, many Buddhists are comfortable with gender flexibility.

One of the texts that describes the rules for Buddhist monks and nuns, called the *Vinaya Pitaka*, tells

Buddhism, like Hinduism, sees gender as a flexible quality. Here, in this painting from a Buddhist monastery in Laos, Lord Buddha is portrayed with feminine qualities.

about two people—one male and one female—who went through a sex change. They went to the Buddha after their sex change, and he allowed them to live as their new gender; the trans-female who had been a man went to live with the women religious, while the trans-male entered into the monastic community. Stories like this one provide an important support for Buddhists today who are going through gender transition.

Buddhism in the United States Today

Because of Buddhism's history of tolerance, today many GLTB Americans convert to Buddhism. People who are both homosexual and interested in spirituality see Buddhism as a much more accepting community than many of the religions in which they were raised.

Like Hinduism, Buddhism's traditions reveal very different perspectives on sexuality from that which most Westerners know. Some of these perspectives can offer help to young adults struggling with their religious identity. Some LGBT Buddhists, however, feel that their religion ignores the issues that are most important to them, and that as a result, their identities are swept under the rug. Sometimes the silence about homosexuality can seem like condemnation.

In Conclusion

Some people would say that much of how we think about sexuality and gender has more to do with culture than with biology—or morality. Not everyone would agree with that statement, however. Others believe very strongly that their religion's absolute code of right and wrong rules out homosexuality as an acceptable behavior. It is a difficult issue, and in today's world, religious people from many faiths are struggling with it.

What do you think?

FIND OUT MORE ON THE INTERNET

Buddhism and Homosexuality
www.buddhanet.net/homosexu.htm

An Introduction to Homosexuality in Theravada Buddhism
www.enabling.org/ia/vipassana/Archive/T/Trembath/buddhism
AndHomosexualityTrembath.html

READ MORE ABOUT IT

Faure, Bernard. *The Red Thread: Buddhist Approaches to Sexuality*. Princeton, N.J.: Princeton University Press, 2008.

Leyland, Winston. *Queer Dharma: Voices of Gay Buddhists*. San Francisco, Calif.: Gay Sunshine Press, 2008.

BIBLIOGRAPHY

Alpert, Rebecca. *Like Bread on the Seder Plate: Jewish Lesbians and the Transformation of Tradition*. New York: Columbia University Press, 2007.

Arrow River Forest Hermitage. "Same Sex Marriage," www.arrow-river.ca/torStar/samesex.html (18 February 2010).

Ellingson, Stephan and M. Christian Green, ed. *Religion and Sexuality in Cross-Culture Perspective*. New York: Routledge, 2002.

Macfarguhar, Neil. "Gay Muslims Find Freedom, of a Sort, in the U.S." *New York Times*, www.nytimes.com/2007/11/07/us/07gaymuslim.html?pagewanted = 1 &_r = 2 (18 February 2010).

Machacek, David W. and Melissa M. Wilcox, ed. *Sexuality and the World's Religions*. Santa Barbara, Calif.: ABC-CLIO, 2003.

Morgan, Peggy and Clive Lawton, ed. *Ethical Issues in Six Religious Traditions*. Edinburgh, UK: Edinburgh University Press, 2007.

Nanda, Serena. *Neither Man Nor Woman: The Hijras of India*. Belmont, Calif.: Wadsworth Publishing Company, 2000.

Norman, Andrew. "Closet Jihad," *City Pulse*, www.lansingcitypulse.com/lansing/article-3790-closet-jihad.html (9 March 2010).

Strauss, Lehman. "Homosexuality: The Christian Perspective," Bible.org, www.bible.org/docs/splife/chrhome/homo.htm (9 March 2010).

Swidler, Arlene, ed. *Homosexuality and World Religions*. Valley Forge, Penn.: Trinity Press International, 2003.

Vanita, Ruth. *Love's Rite: Same-Sex Marriage in India and the West*. New York: Palgrave MacMillan, 2005.

INDEX

ABOUT THE AUTHOR AND THE CONSULTANT

Emily Sanna has a degree in religion from Oberlin College. She went on to attend Yale for her master's degree in divinity. She applies her interest in religion to a wide variety of topics, including GLBT issues and the environment—and even vampires! She has written many books for young adults on topics that range from the lives of hip hop stars to the dangers of illicit drugs.

James T. Sears specializes in research in lesbian, gay, bisexual, and transgender issues in education, curriculum studies, and queer history. His scholarship has appeared in a variety of peer-reviewed journals and he is the author or editor of twenty books and is the Editor of the *Journal of LGBT Youth*. Dr. Sears has taught curriculum, research, and LGBT-themed courses in the departments of education, sociology, women's studies, and the honors college at several universities, including: Trinity University, Indiana University, Harvard University, Penn State University, the College of Charleston, and the University of South Carolina. He has also been a Research Fellow at Center for Feminist Studies at the University of Southern California, a Fulbright Senior Research Southeast Asia Scholar on sexuality and culture, a Research Fellow at the University of Queensland, a consultant for the J. Paul Getty Center for Education and the Arts, and a Visiting Research Lecturer in Brazil. He lectures throughout the world.